UNITY
MAN'S TOMORROW

ROGER SCHUTZ
Prior of Taizé

UNITY
MAN'S
TOMORROW

HERDER AND HERDER

1963
HERDER AND HERDER NEW YORK
232 Madison Avenue, New York 16, N. Y.

Translated from
L'UNITE, ESPERANCE DE VIE
1962 © Les Presses de Taize (S. et L.) France

This translation was first published in England 1962

Library of Congress Catalog Card Number: 63-8518

FOREWORD

Every new situation into which God leads the Christian demands a new spirituality. The contemporary world and our consciousness of Christian disunity raises problems for which we must, turning to the old gospel, find solutions which have never been proposed. But since it is the Lord of history who asks us questions through the events of our time, we have the confidence that the same Lord speaking to us through his Word and his Spirit, will also suggest us the answers.

As a Protestant contemplative, Roger Schutz, the prior of the community of Taize, is especially well placed to announce to us the dimensions of such a new spirituality. As a contemplative he is constantly seeking to listen to God's Word, and as a Protestant, having to justify the life of his community to some of his brothers, he realizes even more than Catholics that Christian spirituality can never be an escape from reality or a flight from responsibility in the world. This book of meditations on unity demonstrates that it is possible to be totally given over to listening to the Word of God and at the same time to be in contact with contemporary problems and have insights into the meaning and the trends of the world which escape a sociologist.

Conscious, painfully conscious, that we are about to enter a new age where a single form of civilization determines the lives of men all over the earth, Roger Schutz seeks the meaning of the Christian calling. We shall completely fail in our task of giving witness to Christ to a world which has become one on the level of science and technology, if we are divided as Christians. Only in our unity can we offer to the world the redemption which is meant to heal the destructive forces which, despite their cultural unity, turn man against man and people against people.

Since we do not now possess this unity, we must constantly seek it. Our quest for unity must formulate our prayer and influence our thoughts and actions. The unity, which is to overcome the barriers sin has erected against man's unity in God, must be built on the unity of the person produced by baptism and the grace of Christ. Unless we strive for the personal unity in which converge the interior and the exterior, the intellectual and the affective, we shall constantly project on the world which surrounds us, even on the religious world, our own inner divisions and conflicts. Ecumenism presupposes peace of heart.

Roger Schutz proposes the notion of ecumenism which has become normative among Protestants, Orthodox, and Catholics who have been in contact, in one way or another, with the World Council of Churches. We take for granted that a Christian belongs to his Church by an act of obedience to his God, and hence no conversation should even suggest that Christian groups adopt changes which compromise their fundamental principles. Ecumenism initiates a movement of dialogue, self-criticism, and renewal in the Churches which will permit the gospel to emerge in the various Christian traditions, purging them from whatever is unauthentic and bringing them closer together in their common heritage. As the gospel emerges more powerfully in the forms of Church life, we often discover, painfully sometimes, that the demands of God go against what at one time we had thought to be essentially related to the Church but which, in the light of the gospel, we discover to be part of our tradition by external custom rather than by inner necessity. Then we must accept the transformation even on the ecclesiastical level.

To make our contribution to the world, we must be positive. We must dare to leave our walls of defense, not because we are strong in numbers—alas, we are not—but because we trust in God. Roger Schutz shows from the principles of the interior life that the Church's mission to announce Christ to the world will be the source supplying us with solutions, which we cannot now see, to the problems of Christian disunity. Unity and mission are intimately related. The wounds of our disunity cannot be healed theoretically: but as we live the missionary life of the Church, which is her most basic form of existence, we shall find the ways of God to become one as he wills.

GREGORY BAUM, O.S.A.
Centre of Ecumenical Studies
St. Michael's College
Toronto

PREFACE

Ever since the beginning of the Industrial Revolution, an insidious illusion has been taking possession of men's mind until now it has become a habit rather well embedded in practice and quite unquestioned by wordly wisdom that big things must be done in a big way; if the world is to be changed, one must plan to do it on a large scale; if the masses are to be affected and the future is to be altered, one must design some kind of universal propaganda sponsered by an international committee and endowed with vast resources. In a world where the quantitative criterion of mass production reigns, everything is made to hang quantitative means.

But such an illusion is sheer deceit, humbug. God is not on the side of the mass propaganda, the largest battalions, although victories of a sort may come that way. In matters of truth and in the realm of the spirit neither numbers nor propaganda really count: A few may change the climate of a generation; a handful may turn the doors of history on their hinges.

It is just such a few, gathered by God's grace from the confusions and longing of this age and bound by a fresh delight in following their Lord in his prayer for peace among his followers, that the brothers of Taizé have 'lighted a candle' which cannot be hid but in this dark world now shines far and wide, making a surer path for many a pilgrim hungry for a larger fellowship than that afforded by the traditional limits of human pride and prejudice inherited in the schism-rent church of our day.

Here in patient, earnest faithfulness to the living God, the path is traced by Roger Schutz, illuminating the steps and barriers which punctuate such a venture to reach again the wholeness of the Church by which it may be at peace with itself and even more significantly, at peace with God.

SAMUEL H. MILLER
Dean of Harvard Divinity School

CONTENTS

PREFACE

LOOKING AHEAD TO THE FUTURE
OF THE HUMAN RACE
God's Today and Man's Tomorrow 13
The unity of the individual personality—a condition of unity between men 16

DISCOVERING THE COMING CIVILIZATION
Technological civilization 23
Mass civilization 27

A CONSIDERATION OF THE POSITION OF
CHRISTIANITY TODAY
The older Christian cultures 32
Areas of missionary enterprise 35
An area of old Christian culture combined with missionary enterprise 38

THE MODE OF OUR PRESENCE IN THE
COMING WORLD
By assuring technological man that he is acting rightly 52
By banishing fear 56
By taking part in the redistribution of material wealth 59
By seeking peace in order to face up to the coming world's distress 68
By visible unity, the condition of our presence in the world 73

SOME DIRECTIVES FOR LIVING TODAY
Keep yourself in God's presence, so that unity may come 85
Do not look back, even at the day just past 89
Let Christ transfigure in us the very shadows themselves 91

LOOKING AHEAD TO THE FUTURE OF THE HUMAN RACE

God's Today and Man's Tomorrow

THERE is only one attitude to adopt if we are going to move forward: we must live in 'God's Today'. Instead of facing 'Today' fearfully, each morning we should welcome this day as it comes to us completely new.

This is still true even in times of trial, for suffering provides an opportunity to take a new step forward into its unknown mystery. Despair dawns only upon a man given up to isolation.

Welcome then each day as entirely new. Tomorrow may perhaps be our last day among men. Without accepting our last day it is impossible to live 'Today'.

If a man looks at 'Tomorrow' as far as it concerns him, he is a prey to anxiety, he is incapable of living in the present and will do nothing but look distractedly in opposite directions, towards the past or the future.

'Tomorrow' must be thought of only for the sake of our neighbour. For ourselves we should live in 'God's Today'. But we must help our neighbour to understand his 'Tomorrow' so that in this way we can help him to enter what will soon be his 'Today'.

We have to look ahead then at man's 'Tomorrow' for the sake of our neighbour, remembering that it will not be in the least like the 'Today' of this generation.

Christians seldom realize that they are at present in calm waters. There is a large-scale confrontation being prepared by a civilization which is coming upon us, and which will break in on us, perhaps gradually submerging us, wave after wave, or perhaps suddenly engulfing us in its rising tide before we know where we are. All that is asked of us is that we just try to keep our heads above water. That is perhaps all we can do to avoid being completely drowned!

Of course the reaction of our time-worn Christian groups might be to turn inwards on themselves and live in Christian ghettos submerged beneath a thousand fathoms of water. But where would then be the radiance of Christ who transcends all civilizations?

Our thinking must be directed towards finding a way for Christ himself to transfigure this new age. But this is an immense undertaking and Christians are in such a weak condition to engage in it—divided as they are. 'Yesterday' they were separated from each other but 'Today' they must rediscover their unity so that the life of God can shine out through them onto this new world.

There is a tendency displayed on a world-wide scale to-day towards a general levelling up of society in the social, economic and technical spheres. This confirms the belief that a civilization common to the whole human race and covering the whole earth is speedily coming into being.

Who then more than Christians should be able to understand this turning point in the history of mankind? Who better than they should be able to adopt a civilization which is to spread to the whole race. The eleventh hour is upon us—an hour when the meaning of that universality and catholicity affirmed by God in Christ should be finding its full achievement.

The structure of our life is going to be fundamentally changed in the years to come. It therefore is up to us Christians to foresee how to orientate the thinking of those who, far from letting themselves be bypassed, actually want to adopt this new way of life which is coming upon us. Our contribution will be in proportion to our capacity. Each Christian must give according to his strength, to the limit of his possibilities. He must overcome the feeling that he can give nothing. If it is true that this turning point in history is serious for a Christendom broken into fragments it is also true that the means of reaching men who are unable to believe, have never been so great.

The unity of the individual personality— A condition of unity between men

ALL that goes to make up the human personality is founded on the indivisible unity of an organism in which body, mind and spirit form a complete whole. The breakdown of any one of these elements—the mind for example—brings on a disorder which affects this indivisibility of the whole personality.

We need to be continually trying to find this unity if we are to achieve and maintain this balance of the human person—trying to co-ordinate our thinking and our action. This balance is achieved just in so far as we have a will to progress stage by stage in a consistency with what is best and deepest in ourselves.

For the Christian the way to such unity is by harmonizing his actions with the thought of Christ who lives within him, by living the faith he professes.

Every quest for unity among men implies first of all that a man who is engaged in it is careful to see that he has this unity in his own person. It would be putting the cart before the horse if one wished to inverse this order. Just in so far as we can overcome the disintegration which threatens us day by day by such inner unity of ourselves, so it becomes possible to work for unity between men and to await eagerly the visible unity of all Christians in one Church.

Unity among Christians therefore presupposes that we are agreed on the prior necessity of each man being at one in himself. This unity of the person cannot be set aside without serious consequences. That is why if a man breaks a solemn promise made in marriage or on becoming a priest—a life promise made before God and man—he always breaks something within himself, even though he does not admit it. The reason for this is that such a broken promise affects the whole personality at its deepest level. Unity of the personality presupposes a man's fidelity to his initial solemn promises so that on every occasion he is able to take upon himself his big personal decisions.

No good is done however by our hiding from the fact that the unity of the person has been destroyed by the 'Separater', the 'diabolos'—the Devil. Man had a stamp on him from the beginning of his creation by his being related to God in unity and he carried in himself this perfect image of his unity, this image of God. Since then every man consciously or unconsciously has been trying to find this lost unity.

Man, divided in himself, is divided too in his relations with his neighbour. Because he lacks this personal unity there quite often arises from the very depth of his personality the need to assert himself against someone else—the need to separate what should be united. So too Christians set themselves in opposition to other Christians, sons of the same Father—and they do this sometimes with all the justification of a confessionally good conscience!

But the call to Christian unity is transforming this situation of ours—now under the power of these forces of disintegration.

Of course the unity of Christians is not an end in itself. It is true that it will be an enormously joyful thing to find ourselves together again, able together to praise the same God. It will indeed be the joy of heaven on earth—this day of our visible reunion in one Church! But that is not the immediate goal. At present the essential thing is to make real the last prayer of Christ on earth. As he foresaw our divisions, and was well aware of the fact that the depths of the human heart are attracted to oppositions and division, Christ prayed to his Father before his departure—'that they may be ONE so that the world may believe'.

To be ONE so that the world may believe! Unity is not an end in itself. Christ did not only pray 'that they may be ONE' but he went on to pray 'that the world may believe', that is to say that by their unity the world may be given the possibility of believing.

To be ONE so that the world may believe! There are two steps here: the first—for us Christians to reunite, the second —for us to unite so that we can bring God to those who do not believe. It is this second step which is going to occupy our interest. It aims at making Christ present throughout the whole world, to men of all races and languages. At the same time it gives us back our first vocation—a vocation which is universal, ecumenical and catholic and given to every Christian in his baptism. Because of our division this vocation is often extinguished, or at least asleep. But where-ever it shows itself it becomes a powerful means of reawakening Christians all over the world.

As soon as we raise the great question of our divisions in the world at present, as soon as we want to make real the prayer of Christ in order to go to this world of our century we are faced with enormous questions which are too much for us and which some of us often misconstrue. As we become aware of them they could overwhelm us by their very size.

Whether we like it or not a new civilization—a new type of man is coming into being. Whether we want it or not this turning point in the history of our time is going to take us into situations where we will be faced with realities which are totally unlike those of the civilizations in which we have grown up. This new civilization which grows apace, which is steadily gaining ground and which by an inevitable move forward will go on gaining more and more—this civilization throughout the whole of the working classes is also on the search for a world-wide unity.

It is because of this fact that the biggest question of this century facing Christians is this: In what way can we realize our vocation to what is universal, catholic, world-wide? How is it possible to go to this world, which in its own way is longing for a world-wide brotherhood and yet still remains so alienated from the Christians?

———

But we cannot go to meet this world with mere goodwill —that would be ineffective and also quite dangerous for us. Before undertaking anything we need to pause; our first job is for each and all to examine clearly the world of today and the world which is coming upon us.

In the following pages we are going to try and discover the nature of this imminent civilization with its two main characteristics: technology and 'the crowd'.

After that we shall consider how the Christians are placed in the world today.

Thirdly, we shall attempt to show a way of maintaining an ecumenical presence of Christians which will allow us without fear to wait for and face up to our responsibilities in this new world.

In conclusion we shall return to some basic principles of ecumenical spirituality that must penetrate to the very depths of our being, so that we can act generously in the world and Church of 'Today'.

DISCOVERING THE COMING CIVILIZATION

Technological civilization

WE have already entered on this new age of technology. We no longer even think about some of its results. When we press an electric switch in our bedroom or when we put our foot on the accelerator of our car, we do not ask ourselves any questions about such things!

All the same, and it is just this which interests us, we are aware only of the dawn of this civilization and we can only guess the sort of man that is going to emerge from it—technological man, 'homo technicus'.

Some examples may help us to identify this world of technology. They could be chosen from the United States or from certain districts of Western Europe, but in these places the industrial revolution happened long ago. There is a country however where everything has begun from scratch recently.

In Asiatic Russia, in those vast regions where there was nothing at all twenty or twenty-five years ago a civilization is coming into being which we can think of as being a type of the one to come. A new type of man is being produced there and he has characteristics which are in many ways identical with those of man in the great industrial centres of the northern United States.

At the beginning of the second World War the industries of western Russia had to be transported to eastern Russia, and so, in this territory which was up to that time almost uninhabited, there are now little islands of the world of technology.

Lack of manpower made itself felt in a terrible way in this virgin country and men were driven to mechanize on a massive scale. Even though they attracted three million labourers a year this was insignificant in the light of the unlimited possibilities of the area. Only by using automation and all the technical means available could they hope to exploit even partially these incredible resources.

So it was that south of Lake Baikal, a new artificial lake was constructed which will produce 24 billion kilowatts of power, the equivalent of the energy of 240 million men— that is to say more than that of all men in European and Asiatic Russia combined. Moreover, they are in process of harnessing the power of the great rivers of Siberia.

We could look for other examples of this technological transformation by going sixty miles inside the Arctic Circle. At Igarka, a village which in 1929 consisted of fifty or so political deportees, there are today 50,000 inhabitants who live entirely from the results of technology and are completely dependent on it. Their houses cannot be constructed in the same way as ours. If they were they would collapse when summer came because the soil which is frozen nearly all the year round thaws on the surface during the summer. Houses and roads have to be lighted during the long winter months. Gigantic greenhouses have to be built to provide greenstuffs for the inhabitants. A town, dependent so much on the resources of technology has been created there because men wanted to exploit the immensely rich forests which had remained unproductive for centuries. The timber of this region is transported from this little port across the Arctic Ocean.

Examples almost as striking could have been cited from the United States. In Detroit, for instance, in fifty years or so the conditions of life have changed completely as a result of the huge complex of metallurgical industries and the gigantic motor works now set up in this city.

It does not matter much from where the examples come. What interests us is that in this technological climate a new type of man is seen to be emerging—a man who is overwhelmed by the sight of the horizon of plenty which is now opened up by the inexhaustible possibilities of technology—and yet a man who, because of this, no longer experiences a thirst for God. Even where faith has remained alive, technology comes to disintegrate a man's religious sense, without his knowing it.

This new man is certainly subjected to strong tensions. There is a division, a break, between his environment at work and at home.

On the one hand, in the public part of his life which he is obliged to assume, he enters a sphere of anonymity. If he is to get on, he needs to acquire a 'personality', and continually to suppress his emotions and rely on what is natural and objective.

On the other hand, his family becomes a place of refuge where public life is rejected. In this setting a man can find a compensation. He can now express a whole side of his personality which had been unable to develop. This is why the younger generation holds the family in such high regard —why they take such a positive attitude towards marriage. They marry while still very young and they will marry at an even earlier age in time to come.

The underlying reasons which enable a man to survive in the world of technology are bound up with the satisfaction which a sense of power brings. First of all a fair-size wage is paid for work requiring skill and intelligence. It is also exciting to take part in forming a new society—it is exhilarating to be bound up with a rising civilization.

Nevertheless the big question facing the coming generation will be about the attempt at readjustment. The new generation will have a new awareness of public life. But in adjusting themselves to this life, youth will reject more and more all interference from traditional groups—whether it be the conformist pressure of the schools, or the influences of traditional politics, or even that of their parents.

If people are going to adapt themselves to this civilization, they will need to be realistic, they will need to face up to the truth.

Mass-Civilization

THE demands of technology give rise to great conglomerations of people in some parts of the globe.

Thus in Great Britain, which was the first country to enter into this technological civilization more than two hundred years ago, a country which for a long time jealously kept its discoveries to itself, more than 80 per cent of the population live in urban centres. Less than 20 per cent are in rural areas.

In the United States some facts are more like dreams! At the beginning of the century Los Angeles was a city with a population of one hundred thousand. Today it is a metropolis of more than six million inhabitants, and this fact is not unique in this vast country.

In Asiatic Russia we find that Sverdlovsk in the Ural region had a population of six thousand in 1860 and today has more than two million, two hundred and fifty thousand.

It would be possible to multiply examples of this population increase in different parts of the world, a growth which is taking place under the pressure of technology.

Some observations can be made about this civilization of the 'crowd'. It makes for a kind of levelling-up of society. Such a regrouping of society into large masses of population will make it more and more vulnerable to the pressures of opinion to which the crowd will want to conform.

Another observation can be made: any country which wants to slow down its birth rate in view of its increase of population runs a great risk. All limitations of the growth of population precipitate not only a serious material crisis for the nation but also a moral one. Any slowing down in the increase of the birth rate is equivalent to a regression—which means to say in the view of some sociologists that the human race is destined to a continual increase.

Moreover it seems to be true according to the findings of some scholars that all systematization of birth control is matched by a corresponding weakening of religious capacity —or translating it into our terms—of the Christian spirit.

A final observation even more significant: Technological man incorporated into these huge conglomerations of population thinks that his effort will have succeeded when a better balance of the division of wealth has been established. This is true no matter which system or ideology obtains—whether right or left. Under the pressure of events the great economies of the liberal and socialist countries will be levelled out to meet one another some day. The East and the West both know today that the game will be won by the side which can transform technically the underdeveloped nations at the fastest rate. The greatest race of all history has begun for the distribution of material wealth.

A CONSIDERATION OF THE POSITION OF CHRISTIANITY TODAY

Moreove
temporary
to look fc
soever.

For the
time is es
something
that they
ities now
civilizatio
terms of

The Ch
with the
consists i
in the r
potential
America
society.

The ob
become
What th
faith, an
He th
us
he
in
nal
ny
the

A ND now what about Christians? How are we placed as regards the advent of this new age, with regard to such profound changes in human society and in man himself?

A careful and clearsighted look at the contemporary Christian world is required. For the sake of clarity we are going to divide Christendom into three areas. First, the older Christian cultures; next, the areas where the faith is being planted by missionary enterprise; and finally, Latin America which combines the characteristics of the two other areas—which is why we give more space to a consideration of this continent.

Thus one may well fear that there could be in North America a sort of new religion that would be the apotheosis of one kind of society and its values or else an idolatrous worship of man. All this is in flagrant opposition to the teaching of the Bible, rejecting as it does all religious 'narcissism'.

All the same on this subject of North American Christians it is important to emphasize the joyful welcome they give you, their hospitality, their generosity, which contrasts with a certain puritanical reserve of European Christians.

As to Western Europe, its characteristics are spiritual apathy and a decline in religious practice. In the Scandinavian countries, as also in a large part of England, only 3 to 8 per cent of the population attends church on Sunday, and the same is true of certain districts of Spain.

In spite of this apathy there are already visible signs of great hope. A Christian élite—an informed body of laymen as well as pastors is coming into existence. Pastoral awareness of priests and ministers is becoming more and more sensitive. Certainly this old continent of ours has never known such quality and strength of pastoral activity, or such a generous, open laity ready for commitment.

In Eastern Europe it is a fact that the closer one gets to the frontiers of the West the more one finds countries with a large Christian population where the life of faith is real. Th in Poland cohesion of Christians in this country is one of more remarkable facts of the Church today. Moreover Hungary there is a vitality of Christian life quite exceptio for Europe. Exception should be made for East Germ where the phenomenon of dechristianization is on increase.

Areas of missionary enterprise

IN these areas Christian groups are numerically feeble, dispersed and divided. Such groups are to be found especially in Africa and, in an even weaker condition, in Asia.

After more than a century of missions the results are very meagre. Out of a population of 216 million in the whole of Africa there are only 13 million Copts of early Christian origin and recent missionary enterprise has produced only 20 million Catholics and 13 million Protestants.

Competitions that has come into play between the various Christian confessions in the continent of Africa is particularly regrettable. Christians coming in on the tide of colonization, brought with them at the same time their confessional positions. An African pastor found it possible to say: 'It is because of you others, European Christians, that we are where we are today. You have brought to us the divisions between Christians, and this fact has dramatic results for us in the present explosive situation!'

These same Christians have to face today two great difficulties. On the one hand, they have to make it plain that becoming a Christian is quite independent of any political position or of membership of any nation or race; on the other hand the white minorities have to place themselves at the service of the African churches. In fact while there is for these groups of European origin a real temptation to withdraw into themselves, there are fortunately some Christians who are aware of their special vocation in this situation.

Here as elsewhere the great wave of technological civilization threatens to swamp these Christian groups. Industrialization, necessary for the country's development, and for the legitimate satisfaction of needs created by Western habits of life, attracts whole crowds of natives to the cities. In Africa Christianity is chiefly a 'rural' Christianity and is in no way prepared for the demands which the situation in the towns makes on it. The African, deprived of his spiritual shelter because his native culture has collapsed, does not find in the Church a real community which is capable of receiving him.

Segregation, which is being accentuated in some countries, has multiplied the number of tiny Christian groups. South Africa in 1954 listed more than a thousand groups, without any connection with one another, and totalling eight hundred thousand members, separated from the missionary churches. All of these have the features of fervent nationalism, proclaiming the messianic longing for an earthly paradise for Africans. These movements have a strong influence; they give to the African the chance to organize a new society to replace the old forms of community life which have disappeared. Moreover, the present generation of African Christians often have only a nominal faith—looking back to the story of their parents conversion—and are not rooted in their own. Many of the baptized are being alienated from their faith by the demands of a strict morality to which the missionaries exhort them.

Since the readiness to listen to the faith is so easily replaced by the different appeals of nationalism and of social programmes, Christians, far from trying to set themselves in opposition to the African in their different confessional alliances, should start feeling a sense of urgency for unity.

In Asia out of 1,700 million there are only 13 million Protestants, and 33 million Catholics (of which 17 million are in the Philippines).

In China and India, the two most important countries of the world in terms of population, Christians are at their weakest. China, with a population of 700 million today, which will undoubtedly be a billion by 1980, has not even 4 million Christians. In India, of the 440 million inhabitants there are about 7 million Catholics, 5 million Protestants and 1 million Orthodox. Of these 13 million baptized 5 million live in the state of Kerala alone, and the other 8 million are spread over the 440 million Indians.

Other Christians in Asia can be numbered at a few million —Christians in the Near East and in Asiatic Russia. It is to be noted that both in Asia and in Africa, there is a discernible growth of conversions in the countries that have recently become independent.

An area of old Christian culture
combined with missionary enterprise

THERE is nothing more thought-provoking for the present ecumenical task than the situation of Christians in Latin America. It is important to give this a fuller treatment than we have given to the other areas because this continent presents, under a magnifying glass as it were, our failures and our hopes and from it we can learn to examine ourselves.

Catholicism

As far as the general public is concerned, to be a believer is to be a Catholic. Introduced into the country with Spanish and Portugese colonization, the Catholic Church has suffered some severe blows in the last two centuries.

The following facts have undoubtedly contributed to a deterioration of Catholicism.

(1) In the eighteenth century, the expulsion of the Jesuits deprived this continent of many competent missionaries who had often known how to adapt themselves to the native Indians and who had on occasions come to the defence of the natives' rights over against the colonials.

(2) During the wars of independence in the nineteenth century, Catholicism underwent a severe persecution at the hands of radical elements who resorted to violence in order to obtain a separation of Church and State. Blood flowed for a century and the consequent weakness was considerable. The Catholic Church finding itself deprived of State support has had to appeal to the wealthy classes to keep its organization going. This fact is going to weigh heavily on Catholicism because it gives a preponderant influence to a tiny portion of the population—the big landowners.

(3) Since the beginning of the twentieth century the Catholic Church has not been able to keep up with the growth of population. In 1900 this continent (in which Mexico must be included, since it is Latin by its language) had a population of 70 million. In 1960 this was 200 million and 500 million are forecast by the year 2000. This is the greatest population increase in the world.

Unless we bear in mind the trials of Catholicism in Latin America over the last two hundred years, we run the risk of complete failure to understand it. This Catholicism which was once so full of vitality has experienced a great loss of strength and has suffered a great spiritual decline.

Today more than a third of the Catholics of the world live in Latin America, yet they have scarcely one-tenth of the Catholic clergy of the world. Much of the crisis in religion comes from this disproportionate state of affairs. There are only forty thousand priests and religious for the whole of Latin America, half of them are foreign and several hundred priests come every year to fill up the vacancies. For a long time now western Catholicism has been coming to the help of their South American brothers.

The percentage of practising Catholics is very low. 3·5 per cent of the men and 9·5 per cent of the women. In the light of these facts Bishop Cambron of northern Brazil writes: 'The majority of my people do not really believe. They are baptized but they have not heard the Word which gives faith . . . By baptism they have been prepared to believe, but they are deprived of what is necessary before they can believe with conviction.'

In spite of this, signs of new life are evident especially since 1955, and they are full of great promise. Effort is being directed toward the creation of new parishes, living Christian communities, and dioceses. In Argentina alone, eleven dioceses have been created between 1957 and 1961.

Christians are becoming aware of the desperate material and moral poverty of the people. Many bishops are taking part in one of the most essential reforms—the redistribution of land. Half the population is rural, but even so 75 per cent of the people of this continent suffers from malnutrition.

There is an exodus of population from the countryside to the cities, which are often quite magnificent in their bold architecture. The peasants huddle together there, wretched parasitic conglomerations of humanity without water, without sanitation, without electricity, without police, who do not dare to go where the law of the jungle reigns with its train of tragedy, the chief victims of which are women and children.

Small rural landowners are comparatively rare. In Uruguay, for example, sixteen big landowners control one half of the productive land.

Bishop Ballon of Peru, following up the papal encyclical *Mater et Magistra* on the occasion of a recent 'Church and Society week' wrote: 'In the semi-feudal system of Peru, private property is the privilege of a minority. It is a complete contradiction to wish to defend the right of private property without insisting at the same time on the distribution of this property among the greatest possible number of people.' After going on to ask for the nationalization of certain large enterprises, which give too great a political and economic power to the few, and moreover, having requested that certain private property be expropriated and redistributed and that a real trade union movement be set up, he concluded: 'Effective action on the part of the Government is urgent. Any government which really represents the common good should limit the right of private property and see that it fulfils its proper function in society.'

The council of the cardinals, archbishops and bishops of Latin America (known as the CELAM) also took its part in all this by declaring: 'We must not forget that two-thirds of the population of the world and of Latin America suffer from economic underdevelopment and hunger. This state of affairs constitutes the greatest sin and the gravest danger of our time.' Such is the stituation of the human race as it is illustrated by conditions in this continent that we may well ask whether the world is going to get on with its task with or without Christians.

Among the bishops who are leading a religious revival is Monseigneur Larrain, Bishop of Talca in Chile and secretary of the Episcopate of the South American continent. As he looks for ways of fulfilling his pastoral work so that there may be a revival of Christianity in the continent, he wishes first of all to emphasize the preaching of the Word. He cites Cardinal Bea on the subject: 'A priest who was solely concerned to celebrate the sacraments but did not make it his job to break the bread of the Word, would only be half a priest.' After having referred to the words of so high an authority in the Church, the Bishop of Chile points out that the diaconate was instituted by the primitive Church so that more time might be given by the apostles to the preaching of the Word. He concludes: 'The secret of an effective pastoral ministry among the faithful is a faith enlightened and nourished by the Word of God and by a great fidelity to the Eucharist'.

Monseigneur Larrain goes on to deal with Church Activities —some which are described as 'works of charity', are a sign of non-Christian attitude, the very opposite of what is intended. Certain so-called means of evangelism are actually ineffective and he gives as an example the immense sums of money spent each year in Chile on small religious publications which are of no value. What then would be an effective way of witnessing? The Bishop of Talca is not afraid to declare that it is the way of poverty, for this is imperative, especially in underdeveloped countries.

The bishop in conclusion speaks of the role of the parish. He calls it the cell of the Church. Now a cell is a basic form of life and cannot simply be an administrative or bureaucratic affair. The pastoral ministry of love, therefore, in the parochial set up will consist essentially of the creation of a Christian community at the centre of every structure of human life.

At this point Catholics and Protestants meet. The important thing is to create parish communities round a man of God. These communities must be self-sufficient from the point of view of material needs and must also give assistance to the very poor. Such parishes would thus quickly become mature because they would be sharing in the building up of the Church on the local level without the help of the wealthy.

In Santiago the most able priests are being sent into the heart of the slum areas.

Protestantism

Because of Protestantism's division into such tiny fragments, statistics about numbers are difficult to collect. In 1938 there were a million and a half Protestants; in 1961 there were nearly 9 million, with sixteen thousand missionaries and pastors for them. Protestantism is divided into nearly three hundred Churches and missionary societies, the majority of which stem from the United States.

There are two kinds of Protestantism here—that of the historic Churches, which are linked to European traditions or to the pietism of the older American Churches, and on the other hand a new kind of Protestantism, mainly imported from the United States—now supported by a considerable number of missionaries who have been driven out of China.

The accent is placed on preaching and knowledge of the Bible. The radio is used a great deal for this and has an importance greater than in any other continent. Two thousand programmes are broadcast every week, sent out from nine private stations.

If the practice of religion is weak in the historic Churches, which represent a third of Protestantism, by contrast it is lively among the new Churches. The preaching of the latter is basically moralistic; the faithful have to abstain from smoking, from drinking alcohol, from dancing and from going to the cinema. There is a whole system of teaching here which is doubtless not very easy for us to understand.

The evangelicals find themselves faced with a crowd of people who are poverty stricken, who await deliverance and adopt towards it a strong messianic longing. So the recently imported Protestantism emphasizes conversion—the moment when a man receives faith—and particularly backs up its preaching with healing by faith and prayer. A serious question arises therefore: the absence of continuity in these Christian groups who are more concerned with producing conversions than with ecclesiastical structure. They get in touch with a huge crowd of people—they kindle a fire at a certain spot and when this fire goes out, when hope is disappointed these same evangelists can always find another

44

great crowd of people and can begin again. The emphasis placed on healing among a people who are waiting for deliverance could lead to a deep disappointment which could discourage even trust in God. One wonders what will become of so many evangelistic efforts which want to live only by the bursting forth of the Holy Spirit in the midst of men.

As an appendix to this problem we draw attention to the fact that the Spiritualists, whose influence is on the increase, also back up their preaching with the hope of healing. Their progress in Brazil is staggering. Sixty per cent of the population frequent their meetings while continuing to be Catholics or Protestants. The Spiritualist, whose forms of worship have often assimilated African and Indian elements, possess hospitals and schools as well as places of worship.

––––––––

A majority of Protestants show an aggresive attitude towards Catholicism. There are many Protestants who, in view of the tensions which cause oppositions and will go on doing so among Catholics themselves, are hoping for a sort of break-up of Catholicism. This raises the question for us as to the ecumenical attitude of Christians facing concrete situations in their own country. What is happening in Latin America is significant. For what we see breaking out there fairly ruthlessly may be able to throw light on our own situation in the old continent of Europe where everything takes place undoubtedly in a more subtle way.

Let us take a look at the sequence of events in the life of the Catholic Church in Chile during the last forty years. By 1920, the persecutions which the Church in Chile had suffered left it in a state of great weakness. What remained of the Catholic Church was supported by the conservative party, while on the other side the radical elements fought against everything that Catholicism represents.

In 1923 appeared a famous letter of the Bishop of Santiago. 'It is clear', he wrote, 'that the Church cannot tie itself to any political party without compromising the supernatural nature and universality of its mission'. Another bishop answered by affirming on the contrary the obligation of Catholics to fight on the side of the conservative party. The question is resolved only ten years later by Cardinal Pacelli (later Pope Pius XII), who took up the argument of the Bishop of Santiago and wrote: 'No party can pretend to represent exclusively all the faithful. Therefore the faithful must be given the freedom to form different political parties and take an active part in them, the only condition being that these parties offer a sufficient guarantee for what concerns respect for the rights of the Church and of souls.'

From that time onwards there began to appear a Christian democratic party, which, while it is still a minority, takes up increasingly bold positions. A great movement towards openness with regard to social problems and a renewal of Church life is being displayed with the birth of the Catholic Action. Monseigneur Larrain, Bishop of Talca, is one of the moving spirits of this recovery.

Tension within Catholicism grows. Certain staunch conservatives accuse the bishops of meddling in politics. When strikes broke out in 1954, even though the right to strike is denied by the Constitution, some bishops began to support the strikers who were demanding higher wages. While the Government was putting the leaders of Catholic Action in prison—the first Christian trade union was being formed.

The reaction of some Protestants to this tension was to begin to wish for a split within Catholicism itself. According to the ideas of puritanical Protestantism it is better to have a Church numerically small, purified of the half-hearted and the well-wishers, freed from the old leaven of hypocrisy and conformity.

At the heart of Protestant thinking there is often a tendency to prefer divisions—better to separate from men who uphold tradition, the conformists who seem to embody the opposition of reaction, rather than to put up with them.

It is because of not being able or not wanting to pass through a period of crisis together, that they break away from their companions. It is often only from a distance that the results of such a break can be assessed. As for ourselves it will be perhaps in the future that we shall discern and suffer from the heaviest consequences of the centuries of divisions between Christians.

When people pass through a period of tensions in married life or in any other form of Christian community, it is quite obvious that a separation would make for a momentarily relaxed atmosphere. That is why the breaking of a solemn vow is able at first, because of the dislocation which it brings about, to bring real relief—indeed the beginning of a kind of expansion. But some processes which take place in the deepest parts of the personality can only be assessed in the light of a long lapse of time. After a period of feeling all right, an abandoned marriage or priesthood for example can only lead to a serious new crisis unless one deliberately gives up the attempt to maintain integrity and to achieve unity of the person.

It must be recognized that every separation, though for the moment it might do away with tension, is definitely an impoverishment. We therefore cannot wish any Christian, and still more any Christian group, to suffer such an impoverishment. So, to return to Latin America and applying this principle to what is happening there, Protestants, far from playing one set of Catholics against another should respond to a fundamental call of the Gospel by being everywhere a leaven of unity.

In no way must we attempt to break up what already exists, but on the contrary help towards that break-through which will alone allow us to come out of a crisis more enriched and the stronger, we must keep ourselves from false victories which we think we have won when we have imposed our own ideas: This is true Christian realism.

By passing judgement from outside on an old Christian tradition, such as the Catholic tradition of Latin America, we run the danger of pulling up the good grain with the weeds. To detach men from their religious allegiance is to run the risk of taking them out of a sociological situation where the grace of God could reach them freely and run the risk of taking them out of the place where a true faith in the line of continuity might be reborn.

Always we must learn to see the Christian we meet with the eyes of Christ, to reflect on the best which God has given to the other man—for is that not Christ himself? This gaze prepares us to respect and to love the Catholic brother and at the same time to discover in him the unsuspected riches that God himself has given.

THE MODE OF OUR PRESENCE
IN THE COMING WORLD

WHAT is our answer going to be to this new civilization, by what sort of presence are we going to make ourselves felt?

All our thoughts about the great questions raised by this age must be guided by certain principles of the spiritual life.

By assuring technological man that he is acting rightly

THE Church, since it is not tied to any one civilization, must give to those who are the first to enter on this technological age and are using its methods—the assurance that they are acting rightly. It is important for the Church to revise its language or its judgements in order to speak to these men.

Christians during the last fifty years have insisted on the value of professional integrity as in itself a sufficient Christian witness. But this language is not really comprehensible to young people and is difficult for the new mentality to accept. That is not to say that the men of the technological age are at this point less moral than Christians, only there is a lack of agreement as to what constitutes moral values.

Then again in speaking to youth, very often Church people suggest that there is a kind of superiority of so-called cultural leisure activities over other pastimes which are characteristic of the new technological age—such as the joy of speed, or music which has the rhythm of the machine.

Or, again, we speak to the younger generation in an academic language—whereas the youth of today distrusts words more and more. So it happens that the Church circles which love discussions and which suffer from a sort of an hereditary thirst for words, for talking—not to say for verbiage—are not able any longer to reach by words the rising generation. This generation already shows a love for the concrete. It is not a question of proving God by arguments: Youth bases its certainties on certain axioms which are not for discussion.

There is quite a parallel case to be made out in this respect between the mentality of Communist countries and that moulded by technology in the United States or West Germany for example. To the extent that they have not been taken in by habits of conformity which wealth imposes, young people today are capable of commitment, and even of sacrifice if they grasp the precise motives for it. If they realize what is wanted from them they will go anywhere! Thus for example in China the younger generation is often asked to take on an almost superhuman task because something concrete is being put before them which is part of a great corporate effort to achieve aims which are apparently of universal significance.

The Church must therefore assure men that they are acting rightly, she must give them the significance of their immense undertaking, of their self-giving mission—these men who are entering on this new age and who are adapting themselves to it often with some difficulty and who are threatened by the religion of technology.

The new man who is being created both in the East as well as in the West believes in technology because his life depends on it. We have mentioned further back that technology has led the American to make a new religion out of the values which underlie technological society. This phenomenon is independent of any specific political ideology.

Indeed in America, as well as in the USSR, a religion is being born, a religion where once again man makes an idol of man as he admires himself in the works of his own hands, and of his intelligence, in the typical attitude of religious 'narcissism'.

This attitude springs from a civilization which is through and through materialist. It is not peculiar to Marxism whose theoreticians, for seeing what a technological civilization means, have expressed in their way the results that follow and have tried to give it an ideological framework.

The Church, however, if she is not tied to one civilization, must know how to teach without giving a bad conscience to this technological man who is so frail and vulnerable and who has such great difficulty in believing in what he cannot see.

The Russian Orthodox Church recently has set up a very remarkable example. A declaration of the Patriarch and Metropolitans of this Church stated that they accepted the science and technology of Soviet society and that the only thing they rejected of the Soviet system was the denial of the existence of God 'which is in any case outside of the competence of science'. This declaration immediately caused a stir in anti-religious circles. Some people affirmed that if the Orthodox Church upheld science and technology, it would be difficult to go on opposing her.

Is it necessary to go still further in order to reach the man of the technical age in the sphere of faith—to adapt Christian prayer to his present horizon? In these days where we breathe in rationalism with the air, the continual tendency is to secularize ecclesiological values. Some go as far as to think that what remains of the scaffolding of Christianity must be destroyed and all that is traditional put in question in order that it may be possible to reconstruct it entirely afresh. They would like to secularize worship itself in order to get in touch with technological man.

But the Russian Orthodox Church here again gives us a very valuable example. By its liturgy, it lives and creates the joy of heaven on earth. The winds have blown on this Church but the prayer of the people of God has remained alive in its places of worship. This prayer which has come down across the centuries, this prayer which not only makes its appeal to the mind but which unifies a whole set of visible and tangible symbols.

What we need to know is that technological man, as he lives with the anonymous rhythm of his work, finds once more precisely here in the age-old prayer of the Church in the homeliness of the house of God, the thing which is lacking in his daily life. So the man who is deprived of all sense of homeliness in his public life is going to recover through actions and expressions which bear no relation to what he sees in his daily life the thing which his personality lacked, so that he can develop into the fulness of the Christian life.

If we only present this new kind of man with the witness of an upright decent life he can say to us: 'You are not offering me anything very different from the life I already lead. What is the use of that? My conduct is just as good as yours'.

And in fact we must show visibly something of the transcendence of Christ to this man who is needing a supernatural joy so that he can regain his balance—he needs the joy of heaven come down to this earth of ours.

By banishing fear

IN this confrontation which is coming we are asked to 'pray that these things do not happen in the winter', which is to say that nothing may be too cruel, too violent, that there should not be too many victims among the weak of this world.

But we cannot live in fear. The man who wants to work for unity, and with this in view wishes to become part of the coming civilization, must first of all shut out fear. When a man's foundation is God he has nothing to fear. He is sure of victory before he starts.

This means first of all not using up or strength by fighting against ourselves within Christendom. It is important to give up the unhappy habit of putting labels on everything, of putting Christians in the categories of 'progressive' or 'conservative' and thereby putting them out of count without realizing that by doing this we are already destroying something of the very body of Jesus Christ. A man does not attack this body with impunity!

To be victorious means too that we do not use our strength against others outside, against those who do not believe or even against the mighty of this world. Even if we could unite all the material resources of the Christian world against these men, we would not be able to accomplish anything very much. A crusading spirit in any form, against anyone whatsoever, must be given up. We must drive away this quasi-physical fear which gets hold of us when we are confronted by different ideologies. We must never entertain the hope that the reunion of Christians would give them a power capable of knocking out the man who is not one of us.

The Christian, for the sake of that which is in him, must be a man who leads on others with him. He must run towards Christ. He has no more fear.

It is right, of course, faced with different varieties of materialism, for the shepherds to warn the faithful of the dangers which threaten them; it is right that they should be continually finding ways of gathering the flock together. But in this case this is not an immediate reaction on the part of the shepherds to the shock that fear brings but it is something positive done as part of the work of the pastoral ministry which has been entrusted to them.

It is important to keep a cool head, to step back and look at the course of events—so as never to confuse or identify the technological and mass civilization with the ideologies which at present are supporting it in some parts of the world. Even more than outdated ideologies, the Christians of tomorrow will have to face a situation created by applications of technology which we can hardly imagine today.

The oppositions and contrasts between these ideologies and between present-day economic systems will undoubtedly decrease. We are moving towards a levelling-up of standards of life in the East as well as in the West. On both sides there are immense possibilites. In the economic field we will arrive in two or three decades at organized planning of the economies of the world whether they be of the 'liberal' or 'socialized' sort.

The real danger of the new civilization is a spiritual one and is the result of the unparalleled advance of scientific instruction. It is interesting, for example, that one out of every hundred receives higher education in Russia as against one out of four hundred and fifty in West Germany. There are also proportionally twice as many engineers being trained in Russia as there are in the United States.

The real difficulty raised by the technological world rests in the hold exercised by education which is elevated to the rank of a religion. There is a very startling observation to be made: In the cities of Islamic culture in Asia, among the Moslems, who have been nomads up to the present day and are now living in the newly constructed cities, it is just those who pass on to studies at secondary and university level who are being drawn away from their Moslem faith. The result of the great discoveries of science completely bewitch a man; they give him at first a feeling of fulfilment, and use up his awareness of God. However unlikely it may seem, the sending of satellites into outer space prevents a man from thinking of God as Lord of heaven and earth. This is not only true for semi-educated minds. In the East as in the West God is dead for technological man.

It is just here that within Christendom the role of the shepherd, of the pastor, must be found. But the true shepherd, if he is to be seized by panic, can no longer do anything to protect his flock and he will infect them with his own fear. A man who has been called to be a priest and pastor tries to find a way in which the Gospel may penetrate those places where it at present does not exist. The world of technology will not be made open to penetration by the Gospel by our hardening up on questions of principle. Such then will be the work of the generation of Christians to come: free from fear, they will make contact with technological man where he can be found, and henceforth make common cause not against but on behalf of men for whom at present belief is impossible.

By taking part in the redistribution of material wealth

WITHOUT being obsessed by the belief in progress, by a sense of justice which would prevail over a burning love for all men, Christians must listen to the question which is being asked of them in this century —the question of the redistribution of material wealth and its fair division throughout the world. We undoubtedly will be judged by history, in terms of what we shall have done or failed to do in this sphere. Now we are well aware of the difficulty we have in sharing even our surplus with those who have nothing. This has always been one of the most serious problems all down the history of the Church and whenever it is a question of giving a little of what one has, there is always a resistance against it.

In the past the pastors and doctors of the Church have been severe on this point

The motives which have determined the Christian attitude to rights of private property can be partly explained if it is remembered that Christianity developed in the midst of a Roman civilization in which the rights of property were absolute and in which there was the possibility of misuse of personal wealth without any accounting to society.

It was into this civilization that the Church put down its roots. When Christians emerged from the period of persecutions to enter on a period of peace, those who had possessions often tried to find a possible compromise which would appease their own conscience in the sight of those who possessed less than they, the poor, the insignificant.

It was just at this time that the doctors of the Church, very much aware of what was taking place, vehemently opposed this state of affairs and tried both by writing and preaching to emphasize the seriousness of the compromises in which the Christians were starting to get involved. The declarations of the Church fathers are so powerful, and put the Gospel point of view so objectively that it is necessary to be constantly recalling them.

St Cyprian, an eminent Roman lawyer who became a bishop and martyr, declares: 'Everything which God has created was given to us for the use of all . . . No one, then, can be excluded from the gifts and benefits of God, all humanity ought to benefit from them in equal measure.'

Ambrose of Milan wrote: 'The Lord has willed the earth to be the common possession of all; but greed has redistributed the rights of property.' And again: 'Nature has given birth to common rights—it is their usurpation which has given rise to private privilege.'

Chrysostom was even more insistent: 'You rich tell me how you have become rich?—I inherited my property. And from whom did the man who left it to you receive it?— From my grandfather. And from whom did he inherit it?— From his father. Can you, as you go back several generations, show me that your riches are legitimate? No you could not, for the root and origin of them are necessarily tainted with injustice.'

Many centuries have passed since the declarations of the great doctors of the Church, but the question of property and of the distribution of wealth remains. The Church expressed herself again during the Middle Ages. All the economy of the period tended to become more and more a rural economy, the land being the total wealth to be exploited. Neither the lord nor the serf could claim that he was the owner of the land in the sense understood by Roman law; for what was important in the Middle Ages was not possession but the right to use the land, and human relationships depended to a great degree on these conditions of using the land.

Individual liberty was quite often reduced to next to nothing under this complex system of land tenure. Hence came the desire to be free of these over-restrictive ties. Certainly Christian charity played a part in the constitution of new societies—the townships, the free boroughs which were built on land set free from all claims on it. The episcopate for the most part often supported this effort to create free townships. In these towns there soon appeared the rise of the wealthy merchant who used his wealth to the detriment of those who were less well-off. The rich wanted to lend to others the surplus of their wealth so as to earn interest on the money that had thus been lent.

But the Church, throughout the whole Middle Ages had an unparalleled severity against lending money on interest, and as the Middle Ages was a time in which everyone wanted to practice his faith and to receive Christ in the Eucharist, which entailed confession beforehand—the Church had a hold on the moneylenders. Whenever therefore a man confessed to having lent money on interest he was immediately asked to do a penance, and this penance consisted precisely in the restoration of this money which had been falsely acquired. The Jews, who were outside the jurisdiction of the Church, were the only people who could lend out their money on interest. As for Christians, if they disobeyed this interdict, they committed a mortal sin in the eyes of the Church, and if they happened to die without having done penance they found themselves with burial deprived them.

The Church wanted to put into practice both the Gospel, which asks a man to lend without hoping for anything in return, and also the Old Testament which forbids money-lending. Pope Leo the Great went so far as to declare: 'Money-lending is the death of the soul.'

It was not until the great period of the Renaissance that the institution of banking was born. After the Reformation this economic system held sway during the modern period, and the Catholic Church was to abandon the position which she had maintained over the centuries with such unparalleled firmness.

The mistakes and inconsistencies of Christians are a heavy burden at the present time

Today, as it had been from the first era of the Church's life, we are asked to work for a better distribution of material wealth throughout the world.

But are we sufficiently aware of what we look like as Christian nations? In the economic sphere, the countries of the nothern hemisphere, comprising the United States,

Canada and Western Europe, have in their grasp the greatest part of the world's raw materials. Some reputable economists estimate that 60 per cent of the raw materials of non-Communist countries falls to the people of the United States, that means to one sixteenth of the world's population.

In our western society we are shut up in a vicious circle: the more we create needs for ourselves the more we disturb the balance of the economy for others. Some theoreticians believe that we can hope for a level of life identical to that of the United States on a world-wide scale in the more or less near future. However, it is important to notice that with regard to agricultural and food programmes alone it will be necessary to increase three-fold the agricultural production of 1960 between now and the year 2000, because at present two-thirds of the population of the world are chronically undernourished and the population increase is going to multiply what is required. Perhaps the over-production in agriculture of the big countries, which have been organized over a long period, and a large-scale economy could restore the balance to this situation. This must happen. The conscience of the world is waking up to these serious questions.

What is certain is that Christians in a foreseeable future will have to orientate themselves towards a teaching that will remind everyone of the careful or at least the moderate use of the earth's wealth where it is to be found in abundance.

What every Christian must keep in mind is the fact that the world's resources will not allow all men collectively to have a very high standard of living in the near future. The standard of living adopted by so many Christian families in the northern part of the globe cannot be taken as the norm for the world of tomorrow.

The comfortable peoples of the West who see their material income grow at a steady rate are incapable of imagining the very slow improvement or the stagnation of the economy of the underdeveloped countries. This division is becoming worse between the two categories of nations. The special feature of the rich nations is that they are not aware of this split. The special feature of the poor nations is a claim-staking drive, a racial and national aggressiveness towards finding a way out of this impasse.

In Peru, for example, an appeal was made to an organiza-tion for economic research directed by a member of a religious order. It was a question of examing the economic structure and of suggesting a solution which would lead to economic recovery. The results of this sociological investigation showed that all the wealth of the country, the banks as well as the mines, the railways as well as the insurance companies were all in the hands of twenty prominent families. The first reform proposed was that the economy should not be left to be conducted personally by these families without any preconceived plan. But giving up this instrument of power was inacceptable to the interested parties, who were not, however, asked to cut down their standard of living nor to give up their possessions. It seems that man has greater difficulty in freeing himself from the enslaving need of power over his fellow man than in freeing himself from riches. In Peru the initial plan was so watered down and transformed that the authors were unable to recognize it and felt obliged to abandon it.

And then there is India and China! When we were young we used to be lulled to sleep with stories of missionaries, which had led us to believe that these greatly populated countries had swarms of Christians. But now we know that in India there are only 13 million Christians and in China 4 million. Many are dismayed today when they learn that Christianity has been there in some cases for centuries and yet so little has been achieved, and it has left these people in such great material wretchedness. In the last ten years first one and then the other country has launched a five-year plan in the framework of a planned economy, which is very strict in China and more liberal in India. Everyone knows that in ten years reforms have been achieved, in China especially, which would hardly have been credible if anyone had predicted them.

Today Christians may well ask themselves: 'What were our fathers in the faith doing?' Was it not their duty to help towards a better distribution of the material wealth in India and China during the course of the last two or three hundred years? Has such real missionary heroism borne so little fruit? Are the actual results going to be destroyed? Why is it that a better distribution of material wealth is beginning to be undertaken in the parts of the world where we had the possibility of having an influence and where we are at present being pushed out step by step?

What a Christian sees written in the plan of Providence is that just at the time when the growth of the earth's population is being stepped up, the discoveries of technology and the organization on a large scale of industrialization could come to the aid of human needs. The problem to be solved is therefore that of a fair distribution of wealth. Otherwise the economic capacity and power of some of the earth's people, and the use they make of it, serves to exacerbate the feeling of helplessness of the underdeveloped part of the world and drive their people to make themselves heard.

It is astonishing to what extent even the most retarded peoples have a growing thirst for knowledge. Their rising generation wants to acquire a degree of culture which will put them on the level of the more developed nations and give them the means of acquiring our privileges. We can be glad of such phenomena because knowledge given time helps a man to become adult and enables him to put aside reactions based on mere feelings.

Soon competition on a world-wide scale will begin between the various nations who are capable of immediate, effective action with regard to the disinherited nations; that is to say the nations who have not 'inherited' the sort of life as we have. Today, as in the days of the Church fathers, we are being asked to help forward a just redistribution throughout the world of material wealth. Some Christians have already thought about the immediate possibilities. They are open in fact in countries in process of development through the mere presence of Christians who commit themselves to work as technicians in order to help towards the amelioration of material conditions. Their freedom from vested interest is in that case an important part of their effectiveness.

There are only too few Christians as yet who are 'present' in this way. One of them, a Catholic trade unionist of Latin America, Maspero, was able to write: 'Up to the present, freedom means for some people—a minority—freedom to write, to speak, to mix, to carry on trade, to engage in politics, to travel, to invest capital without any sort of hindrance. For the others—the majority—freedom is the possibility of eating, finding work, having a roof over your head and a little security, being respected—being able to stand up for yourself.' As a group, Christians are regarded by the underdeveloped countries as those who have given their consent to the first form of liberty only—so bringing about a complete confusion of values.

The Gospel, which is always stirring up liberating forces and which brings with it at the same time a respect for the human person, can never justify selfish attitudes in the sphere of material wealth. Christians in principle, no matter what hinders them, ought to be promoting a movement towards a system which liberates the human person—which respects human personality. Will they understand too late that by piling up acquired wealth they deprive others of it and that only an economical and a moderate enjoyment of this world's goods can prevent us from being hypocrites. Responding to the invitation of Pope John XXIII in the Encyclical, *Mater et Magistra*, will they agree on the necessity of speeding up certain processes of socialization? One may well be allowed to ask whether Christians who are so slow in entering into the movement of history in the sphere of co-operation will not let themselves be left behind by the children of this world. That would be to accept the conclusion that the world is going to fashion itself without us.

By seeking peace in order to face up to the coming world distress

A MAN can be certain of both receiving and showing forth the fullness of life in God when the peace of God rests on him, penetrates him.

That is why men of the Old Covenant—the men of the ancient people of Israel, desiring as they did to live in God, when they met one another called down peace on their neighbour. 'Peace be with you'—such was the greeting of the Jewish people. It meant 'May peace be on you, may it clothe you, penetrate you.'

This appeal to peace runs right through the history of the people of Israel and after them right through the history of the people of the New Covenant—the Church. But a new fact existed with the New Israel—by the coming of Christ a hitherto unknown quality of peace flows from the reconciliation of man with himself, with his neighbour, with God.

Because Christ has reconciled us, we in our turn have to reconcile all men. And because Christ has forgiven us we must in turn forgive: 'Forgive us—as we also forgive.' This is the new fact: reconciled by Christ, forgiven, clothed in peace, men can now live together in a single body, in the Church.

The peace of reconciliation restores the unity that had been lost and frees man from his natural distress. Divided within himself man wants to do the good which he loves but nevertheless does the evil which he hates. To this divided man is addressed an appeal—to live in the peace of Christ, the source of unity: 'may the peace of Christ, into which you have been called in order to form one body, reign in your hearts'; which means in the deepest part of ourselves—in the most secret depths of our personalities.

The peace of Christ dwells in us every time we reconcile ourselves with our neighbour. Moreover if we are not reconciled how can we approach God, how can we approach his altar? We must leave our gift—however generous it is—which we want to offer to God, and first try and reconcile ourselves with our brother.

This peace of Christ dwells in us every time we are instruments of reconciling our neighbour with God—by forgiveness, by compassion, by tenderness of heart.

There is such a joy for the heart in living for peace, in being at peace with oneself and with God! In spite of the load of cares ever present, in spite of forgiveness which is made more difficult if one has been scorned or humiliated—sometimes by the very Christians from whom one expected a merciful spirit—in spite of all this burden which is there every day, for everyone, there is an unsurpassed lightness of heart which no one can remove from the man who lives by the peace of Christ.

Admittedly, there are some people who seem to be basically troubled, quite incapable of getting out of ruts in which they are, marked with a sense of guilt which crushes them, unable to accept new and bold responsibilities, and finding themselves with the impossibility of living day by day by the compassion and the forgiveness of God. These men and women, laden with the sense of their guilt, are deprived or often deprive themselves of the fullness of the peace of Christ.

Now this peace lives in our hearts—in the very deepest recesses of our being. This means that all ministry of reconciliation has to begin with ourselves so that having been once given peace we are able to bring peace to others.

Ambrose of Milan tells us: 'Begin the work of peace with yourself so that once at peace we can bring peace to others.' So that I can be a peace-bearer a conversion of attitude needs to take place in me. It is only when my sight is completely rectified that I shall see the man before me not in the light of his lesser qualities but above all in the light of the very best that is in him.

So for example in approaching certain high dignitaries of the Church, who from a distance appear to be aloof, whom we believe to be taken up with the weight of authority sometimes inherent even in ecclesiastical government, it is essential to go to these men with the peace of Christ, unencumbered by prejudice, and to be able to see them primarily as men of God carrying on their shoulders the whole pastoral and apostolic concern for the world. For those who found themselves face to face with this pastor, that bishop or archbishop, cardinal or patriarch, this discovery of the fact that their souls are primarily pastoral, and their readiness to see in them the gifts that God has given have allowed them to go a long way in the ecumenical dialogue.

Does such an attitude mean an absence of clear thinking? No. Very simply a man who is trying to find peace keeps his negative judgements to himself. He knows that if he brings them forth to the light of day, he would somehow do an injury to the body of Christ in its visible institution and by the same token without knowing it become a servant of discord.

Everyone in respect of this peace is personally called 'to form a single body' with other Christians according to the apostle's exhortation—a single body: that does not mean any sort of spiritual unity, but one single visible Church. At this point the strongest opposition arises. Peace is a condition of unity. Peace is necessary as the indispensable prelude to this impossible unity of Christians. Everything stands in its way—in me and in others!

In me: My early upbringing has a hold on me, all the habits of life and thought which form part of the depths of a man's personality—and reach to my existence in flesh and blood, everything is opposed to this real communion—to this being in contact with my neighbour.

In others: Will they be able to free themselves from the petrified structures of time-worn Christian groups? There are so many forces, so many resistances which are leagued together without our knowing it.

Ought we not then to give up for good this illusion and to finish with all attempts at the ecumenical quest for visible unity? Yet the apostle joins together in the tightest knot, peace and unity. To accept the first, peace, and to reject the second, unity, would be to make the Word of God into a lie.

So to realize our vocation to unity there is no other way but to walk by faith—treading down all those good reasons which militate against visible unity of all Christians in a single Church.

71

In conclusion, the unity of Christians has to be lived out today. One does not argue about unity—one lives it. Otherwise reasons—good reasons for or against—mount up.

Yes indeed, there are the impossibilities. There are more than enough of them to discourage us. But a discouraged man—unable to 'keep the unity of the spirit in the bond of peace'—such a man cannot be a worker for Christian unity.

So, in order to keep peace it is still essential to live in the present—by feeding on this hope which flows from peace, this peace to which everyone has been called with the purpose of forming one body—the body of Christ, the Church.

By visible unity, the condition
of our presence in the world

INVOLVED in the course of a period of history which sees that the face of the world is changing, our generation needs to stand back and follow the advice of the Gospel, we need to see if we can afford 'to build the tower.'

A preliminary observation is to be made. Time is not very much on our side, and Christianity is getting short-winded and sees the practice of religion diminishing. Nevertheless an immense, a rare hope is given to us.

Certain methods of this very technology are coming into existence to support as never before the missionary activity of Christians. By radio and television, by methods of rapid travel, communication is stimulated between Christians and also with those who do not believe, and this is happening on a global scale. By this very fact we are given an essential factor in guaranteeing the unity and catholicity of the Church.

There is, too, the formation of a Christian élite capable of living not self introverted lives, but shining out and open to the world which is coming.

At the same time we have to remember that the technological and mass civilization brings in its wake a tide of materialism. Men overwhelmed with the almost unlimited material possibilities they can see coming to them are closed to hope in God. Is this civilization going to mean the rapid end of Christianity with its churches spread throughout the world? We are enormously incompetent to undertake any penetration of this world—to be the leaven in the lump!

As we constantly lose ground we are all the time fighting on ground already lost.

Yet the man of today needs the Gospel just as much as the man of the Middle Ages. For just when he feels he has everything this man remains dissatisfied. He has, without knowing it, a hunger and thirst for being close to God. The most fantastic achievements of a new civilization will never quench this thirst and will not cover up with anything the metaphysical disquiet a man feels when faced with his own death.

A new mentality must be matched with new methods. The most part of our methods of evangelization are out of date and usually touch only the people who are already convinced. There are so many efforts with no possible continuity. There is such a waste of generosity. Mere goodwill is not enough for evangelization—some preliminaries are necessary.

Some try at the present time to confront the situation of technology with faith, but they reach in fact only those circles which are already Christian. Many efforts are being made in all directions, but all this seed takes no root for lack of soil. What is missing is a Christian front visibly united so that the world may believe.

A line of demarcation still separates Christians in this respect. One set continues to be satisfied with a spiritual unity—not very demanding in respect of the bonds of brotherhood which should exist between all who bear the name of Christ. For the other set, the visibility of the One Church is a necessary and vital part of its constitution. The acceptance or refusal of visibility will crystallize and determine in the near future the various positions for or against the restoration of the unity of Christendom.

Today so many Christians of course are calling themselves ecumenical! But it is a matter of knowing from what ecumenical perspective a man is looking. Ecumenical work is made up of patience and charity. It's only of any use if we expect our brothers to make steps which they find possible— instead of asking them to make those which their faith makes impossible; if we are ready ourselves to make those that do not contradict our fundamental convictions. It will be effective if we give up all facile ways of thinking as we prove our absolute loyalty in regard to other confessions.

This realistic and effective ecumenism demands a conversion of our attitudes. It is not sufficient to wish for any kind of dialogue with our separated brothers in order to be able to call oneself ecumenical. We need to want this patient dialogue which demands from others the necessary purifications and first of all commits us ourselves to this path.

Because of the division of Christians we are in 'a dry land where no water is.' In the unity of the sacraments and a prayer life which is shared once again in common we could offer to technological man 'that good part which will not be taken away from him.' For when a man, carried along by the fervour of the praying Church, bends his knees before God, even if his prayer has not reached the stage where it becomes explicit, a harmony has been established between rational man and man the image of God.

———

The whole of our thinking in the years to come must come to bear on our simple, practical answer to the problems of witness by a Church visibly one in a divided world. Outstripping the times Christian men and women have tried to join up with the paganized milieu of the great urban centres of the working classes. Out of this some facts are already coming to light.

Rehabilitating the Christian way of life

In a large part of the non-Christian milieu, and, in particular that of the working classes, the Christian way of life has lost its standing. It has to be stated that all the goodwill in the world to lead non-believers to explicit belief ends in nothing, and compared to the enormous efforts that are made there are no fruits worth mentioning. We have arrived at a point where first of all a certain rehabilitation of the Christian way of life is desirable. In the immediate future there has to be sharing of the life of men in the setting where we find ourselves—bringing to it the presence of Christ through our own persons.

This identification with the setting, to which one belongs by deliberate choice, can produce real suffering in Christians who would try to be genuinely the brothers of non-Christians —a suffering which arises from the injustices, sometimes crying injustices with which one meets. These Christians who try to live by the unique, silent presence of Christ may be overcome by a violent feeling of revolt against the Church, against Christians. In fact they find it difficult to accept that their brothers in the faith do so little to banish injustice from the earth.

Now a Christian cannot be overcome by bitterness in his heart and profess at the same time with his mouth the love of all men. There is a profound contradiction at this point.

Hence the first thing to get to work on is oneself: to purify oneself from within with respect to those who are responsible for the injustices, so as to be able, once the bitterness has been consumed and transfigured in the love of Christ, to put forward a just solution which does not spring from reactions such as anger, spite, or discouragement.

Responding to the demand for holiness

Compared to the vastness of what is needed, what we are able to do to serve others is so very insignificant. But let this bit of mutual help always be a sign of love.

In our work and on all occasions of our daily life we need to avoid pushing ourselves forward as if we ought to be doing better than the others. We are, and must remain, ordinary beings on the level of work, of effectiveness, and we ought to know that the extraordinary remains hidden: the invisible demand for holiness.

The people the world is needing are those men who are exceptional for the attention they give because they love. It is saints that the world is waiting for. Such is the secret appeal which rises from the depths of the sufferings of mankind.

Some women, who by their vocation live out this silent presence in a factory, told me that they could not remain unconscious of the advances which were renewed each day by this or that workmate: 'We are constantly being contaminated by the kind of life we live; hence the necessity to have a thirst for the salvation which God gives—for oneself and for others. And one of them added: 'May Christ help me to be converted each day together with them all.'

Only such a demand for holiness is capable of fitting us to live in surroundings on which fall darkness and the shadow of death. More than ever the world has need of saints. In the night of our world there must be men and women like a light of the world, and being this not so much because of their natural as by their supernatural qualities. 'In the depths of my life I can only live from Christ, from a single love—the love of God.' This is how one of these Christian women, who are committed to a difficult life in a factory with all its daily immoralities, expressed herself in a conversation with us.

Renewing our strength within the Church

Life in the midst of the non-believing world is only endurable if a man is firmly incorporated into the body of the visible Church. It is therefore necessary to provide for periods of silence and of renewal in the course of one's life —to make retreats in some community which is visibly united in prayer in the light of the Transfiguration. Such is the conclusion of our researches shared with those who are living out the presence of Christ in the midst of those who cannot believe. Men and women who are worn out need to be restored by the prayer of the Church—to be sustained by the fellowship of those who have the ministry of prayer within the Church. They need to enter into this prayer themselves, committing to God, with serenity and as concretely as possible, all that has piled up in them.

It is plain, therefore, that the world has need of men and women who, without detaching themselves from the work of building the city of man, are primarily in the world as signs of the coming kingdom.

Having an ever deeper knowledge of contemporary society and an armour of solid doctrinal training, but dominated by a sense of urgency, these men and women, married or single, living as they do in the midst of those who do not believe, will rehabilitate the Christian way of life which had been so devalued.

The need will become more and more urgent for these little households of light, scattered here and there throughout the world but united in a single Church. Such could be the missionary scheme which would have most influence in the time to come.

Christ cannot any longer be proclaimed in a competitive situation. In a world of rapid social change can we lose the sense of urgency faced with the world to be evangelized, can we forget the billion and a half of non-baptized in Asia and the 170 million of Africa? While we are advancing in scattered ranks the world is fashioning itself without us. Christians, by a deplorable competition that they set up among themselves in the same missionary locality, some-times use up the best of their energy in condemning or in neutralizing each other. Some go to preach the Gospel where Christ is already proclaimed (perhaps because thus they justify in their own eyes their confessional position as well founded). By such action Christians are forgetting the swift evolution of the world and are in danger of soon being submerged under a thousand fathoms of water in little local churches without any visible unity between each other.

Now if there is no fellowship—and competition does away with any kind of communion—the radiance of the Gospel is compromised in the eyes of all those who are unable to believe.

Of course we shall not end up by leading the whole world to explicit faith. But as we wish the world to fashion itself with us we believe it is necessary to seek to regain our unity first of all and to make of the quest for visible unity an indispensable prelude for Christian mission faced with a world which cannot believe.

While we wait for this visible unity there still remain for our missionary thrust so many vast regions where Christ is not proclaimed. In such places these little households of Christians can go and become agents of transfiguration. On such households of light, scattered throughout the world, by secular institutes, or under some other form of community, depends the very hope for the civilization to come.

These households will take on the non-believing world. In the same way as, according to the apostle, the unbelieving husband is sanctified by the believing wife, so the world which is unable to believe, is adopted, transfigured by some Christians, who are Christ-bearers. However, it is still necessary to provide for this sort of presence.

———

Christian unity requires of us a special attention to the world of today. The task and calling of the young generation of Christians will be to offer all their strength so that they can go to this world, and in order to do this, to bring about a reformation of Christian thinking where it is too limited and partial. This must be done in order to see things on a large canvas—to reflect ecumenically on these great questions which are facing the whole world and therefore to make up for what is lacking in the West, unable as it is to give the rising generation a general vision of things, a large-hearted collective ideal.

The worth of present-day Christians will be in the giving up of their confessional warfare 'in not trying to find out who was wrong and who was in the right', as Pope John XXIII expressed it. That does not mean minimizing the importance of truth and the affirmation of the basic doctrinal positions. But if these real problems were the only thing dividing us we would be nearer than we suppose. This can never be stressed enough.

Moreover, how can we defend the truth if we remain boxed up in our confessional divisions? If there is one certain truth of the Gospel which cannot possibly be denied, it is indeed this unity between those who confess the name of Christ. To defend divisions in the name of truth, and then to go on living in separate sections is to expose ourselves to the risk of losing all authority needed for teaching the basic truths of Christian doctrine. He who is attentive to this unity, which is truth par excellence, and who tries to live it out fully, will speak of Christian truth henceforth with more authenticity.

The union of Christians will certainly not come about by the triumph of one group over the others. If there were to be a victory of one and a defeat of the others no one would accept such a unity. Do not let us try and find out who was wrong and who was right. Let us give up our age-long strife and let us make ready a really missionary Church.

Then we will be caught up on a steady current in order to meet the men of tomorrow. This astonishing process which makes us ambassadors of Christ so as to make him present in the life of men, this undertaking is inspired by the universal vocation laid up in each one of us by our baptism. It gives us back the sense of urgency with which we have to think together about the world which is coming, refusing to work out our own salvation without our neighbour, even when this salvation for each in particular means perfect joy and fulfilment. For it is not in isolation but together that we wish to live in the midst of the life of men and to be the leaven in the lump.

SOME DIRECTIVES FOR LIVING TODAY

Keep yourself in God's presence,
so that unity may come

HOW can each man, at each moment respond personally to the ecumenical vocation? By feeding the flame which has been enkindled for unity all over the world; by keeping himself in God's presence with this intention; alone or in prayer together; on his knees, standing, sitting—it makes no difference! We know that unity is the supernatural work of God and all our activity is not worth anything except in so far as it continues this prayer and makes it real.

To keep ourselves in God's presence is not beyond our strength, does not exceed our human capacity. We can do this even if we are not conscious of any feeling of God's presence, and even in times of loss of fervour, remembering that the objective presence of God does not depend on our awareness of it.

Some people, having gone along this way a long time, will one day perhaps make a new step forward and make an offering of their life to God for the sake of unity.

———

At this point a great hope is dawning: ecumenical encounters on a small or great scale are multiplying. A new awareness of unity is coming to pass and is inspiring large assemblies. As proof of this there are the examples of the preparation for the Pan Orthodox Synod at Rhodes and the great assembly of the World Council at New Delhi.

Within Catholicism, the announcement of the coming Vatican Council has opened up new avenues which will not be closed again. As this council proceeds, will things happen which will have consequences for unity? Of one thing we can be sure—that the Lord of the Church answers the prayers of his people. It is for us to implore the Holy Spirit to speak to the fathers of the council.

It may break forth suddenly—an event which will shine forth on Christians like lightning. And if the event which God brings to pass should happen in the heart of the institution without being visible to bodily eyes, it will not on that account be any the less real.

An attitude which consists in waiting for nothing so as not to deceive or be deceived does not spring from faith—in the ecumenical realm our vocation would then be snuffed out.

Let us be glad for the fact that Catholics are beginning to open up towards ecumenism by the very fact of the preparation for this Council. It is incumbent on non-Roman Christians to tend this flame by their prayer as they live out the pain of division in the depth of a life hidden with Christ.

————

After a long separation we are convinced that God is visiting us at this time and pouring out on us his gifts. He is asking us more than ever to keep ourselves in his presence, to give him thanks for his 'today' and to refuse henceforth to look back on the history of our divisions.

Keeping ourselves in God's presence means letting God penetrate us without our knowing how; it means to agree to his changing our own viewpoint little by little, and giving us the same viewpoint as Christ from which to look at our separated brother, and even at the brother who belongs to the same confession as ourselves. For in so far as we are not looking at our neighbour, and all the more our brother in the faith, with the eyes of Christ, we are condemned to understanding nothing of those we meet.

We are all in the same lump—more than we realize. We are well aware of this at the present time as we meet the same resistance to that for which we stand. And this resistance is offered by a world which, while it is unable to believe, seems to have a better insight than we have into the identity of that which inspires us.

Why should we Christians try to emphasize what divides us? Let us also remember that any argument which comes from pent up bitterness is not the slightest use. Only generous attempts to understand the behaviour of separated brothers can give us the right to emphasize differences between us.

Moreover, it is strange to find how often, on one side and on the other, there is a resemblance, deep down, between certain negative reactions as there is between certain great and high aspirations. The depth psychology of one and the other is marked with the same stamp.

Does not Protestantism itself by its history and origin exist only as a reaction to Catholicism—because of it and in relation to it, in such a way that it cannot radically distinguish itself from it without denying itself at its roots. Whether we wish it or not we are all part of the same lump and that in itself is why we can hope.

This is why today, inspired by an awareness of the Church, and the quest for the visible unity of all Christians, Catholics, Orthodox, Anglicans and Protestants, there are some Christians who, seeing one member of the body suffer, wish to suffer with him—and rather than running away for fear of being contaminated wish for nothing else than to be present to the Church as they wish to be present to the world. In this spirit when they meet Christians in difficulty in another confession than their own, they wish to be active witnesses to unity and hence what they do is to bring them comfort, to help them, to re-establish them gently in the place where they are as they would themselves wish to be. For if today I am standing up—tomorrow I may fall. Who then will come to pick me up?

Do not look back, even at the day just past

ONCE we have considered how fundamental the demand for visible unity is for us, for the Church, for the world, and then having put our hands to the plough, it is no longer possible to go back and look at the humiliations, the wounds of the past, even of yesterday.

Let us take care not to run here and there in the name of unity instead of beginning with ourselves and with those closest to us—in our married life, our family, our parish . . . Married life is imperilled if, by our looking back at yesterday's quarrels, it is not lived in the present.

However, unity does not mean that we buckle ourselves up for introspection. It would be so easy to keep oneself aloof, by calling in highly spiritual arguments. Thus in the name of family, of parish unity, a man could find himself closing in on himself, and that is just the point at which the sectarian attitude begins to creep in.

If Protestants, face to face with Catholicism, look back, if they scrutinize the past or even just the day before, perhaps they will feel a bitterness which is a betrayal of the burning love of Christ. If on the other hand, they consider positively the Catholic renewal, the Protestants can become for the Catholic Church a source of life and not of death, if on that account they loyally give up confessional proselytism in order to spread the sweet smell of the Gospel. These Protestants can be sure in this attitude of faith and charity, that they are fulfilling their true mission and that they will be preparing in the world a revival without parallel.

Let Christ transfigure in us the very shadows themselves

OUTSIDE the light of Christ we are wrapped in shadows. That is true of all of us and will be for ever and ever. Only we are more aware of this at certain moments in the history of our lives or at certain periods in the history of mankind.

If one Easter Eve we went into this or that church in the East or West we would find ourselves in the midst of the faithful who have come in the silence of the first morning just as at the dawn of the resurrection of Christ the women, wrapped in shadows, came to the tomb. When the cantor intones: 'The Light of Christ' and lights a candle in the midst of the faithful they reply, 'Thanks be to God'. And this is repeated three times. It is a thanksgiving for the resurrection.

Now the light of the Transfiguration of Christ means for us that already today the work of the resurrection has begun in us.

The Apostle Peter, who was present at the event, gives us the very meaning of the Transfiguration in one of his epistles. He thereby teaches us a whole aspect of the Christian life.

We are in the night. In the midst of the darkness shines a little lamp. All that is required is to keep our eyes fixed on this light 'until the morning begins to break and the day's star arise in our hearts'.

Why look in the distance for something which is so near? Sometimes when faith and patience are at low ebb we demand signs and wonders, tokens which are immediately visible. But we must look at this light perseveringly before the day star will arise. As we keep ourselves in God's presence we have to see henceforth everything in the light of Christ—to think about our neighbour in this light, our fellow Christian, our own persons and the whole of our life.

We have to think about our neighbour in this light—to know that in every man, even in the man who does not confess Christ, there shines the reflection of the very image of the Creator. Our neighbour is not just the man whom we like but the man whom life has wounded and deposited at the side of our path. He is not only the man for whom we feel an immediate friendship but also the man who just because he is indifferent to us deserves all the more to be looked at with the very gaze of Christ.

To look at a fellow Christian in this light is first of all to see in him a Christ-bearer—and then to give up complaining about everything that we may find negative in him in order to look at the gifts—the positive work of God—the little light that He has placed within him. Nothing renews us as much as discovering the lively hope which is displayed by a witness of God badly treated by life.

We have also to look at ourselves in the light of Christ. Rather than allowing ourselves to stop because there is something bad in us, inabilities, darkness, shadows—there always will be such things—we must know how to put down all this burden by making use of confession, and having received absolution, we live by it immediately; for a man does not live by admitting his sin or by the feeling of his guilt, but in Christ who shines in him like a little light lit up in the midst of the darkness.

Consider all life and see all creation in this light of God since, in its origin, all creation was intended for the very fullness of God himself.

———

A plant which is not turned towards the light withers. In the same way a Christian who refuses to look at the light of God but on the contrary wants to see nothing but the shadows is condemned to a slow death. He cannot grow and build himself up in Christ.

It has been granted to the apostles led up the mountain apart to have a visible token of what is in store for them on the day when they will be one with Christ in God.

Little by little Christ transforms and transfigures in us all rebellious contradictory tendencies, all those troubled states of mind and vexed moments which are still left in the depth of our personalities and over which the will sometimes has no control.

It is possible from now on to assure certain people who are convinced that they have 'ruined their lives', that in the patience of God nothing is lost. Christians as eminent as St John of the Cross and St Teresa of Avila began fairly late to live a new life—two saints who have led so many men and women to Christ and who then speak of the fire kindled with all the wood of their past.

For those who are marked by suffering and by the Cross of Christ, the day will come when they will be able to burn with the fire which is fed by all their past. From that moment they will know that nothing exists without a reason for it— nothing is ever lost in God.

The light of Christ transfigures in us the shadows themselves. These shadows are none the less present and sometimes we can do nothing about them. But then it happens that as the life of Christ slowly develops in us, what was still dark, restless, opaque and even disturbing is peacefully enlightened and taken up into God. Nothing is lost on this earth because God is strong enough to give us back all things, reshaped, changed, revitalized, transfigured by him. However, we do have to wish to turn ourselves towards the light.

Just as the light of Christ does its work in the midst of our inner darkness it also works on the opacity of the world. So God adopts to himself unbelieving humanity: by living in the midst of human beings who cannot believe a Christian is a Christ-bearer; with the utmost discretion he communicates the very presence of God.

The apostles contemplate Christ transfigured and they wish to live in this dazzling light because they know very well that they are living then a climax of their lives. But they have to come down from the mountain and from then on to see the light of Christ shining in the growing Church, in themselves, in the world in the midst of men.

And that is also true for each Christian: he must come back down and radiate the glory of God without noisy words in such a way that, by this light of Christ in us, everyone will have an insight into the very source of our visible unity. By it the man who is not able to believe, without knowing how, will be led towards hope in God.